Sacred Spaces: Architecture and Religion in Historic Wilmington

Exhibition and Catalog Support:

Patron

Tabitha McEachern

Sponsors

Atlantic Printing
The Landfall Foundation

Sacred Spaces: Architecture and Religion in Historic Wilmington

Walter H. Conser, Jr.

Bellamy Mansion Museum
of History and Design Arts,
Wilmington, N.C.
A Stewardship Property of Preservation North Carolina

Cover:
Postcards courtesy of the Bellamy Mansion Museum, McAllister & Solomon Used and Rare Books and New Hanover County Public Library/Local History Room.

Curator:
Walter H. Conser, Jr.

Project Interns:
Blair Jackson and Kristen Ostiguy

Editorial Assistants:
Maggie Noffke and Suzanne Roth

Catalog Design:
Julie Macie / Pixel Sharpeners

Illustration abbreviations

CFM: Cape Fear Museum

NHCPL: New Hanover County Public Library

ISBN Number: 0-9673037-0-2

For Emily, Sam, and Scout...native Wilmingtonians.

Introductory Statement

Walter H. Conser, Jr., Exhibit Curator

Wilmington has a rich architectural heritage. The downtown historic district, one of the state's largest, showcases the energetic work of preservationists and contains an assortment of architectural styles and an array of significant residential, commercial, and religious buildings remarkable for a city its size. The architectural inventory of Wilmington's churches, meetinghouses, temples, synagogues, chapels, tabernacles, and other places of worship is especially noteworthy.

At a glance it is easy to find the excellent examples of religious architecture that Wilmington offers. Home sometimes to the same congregation for many years, other times housing different faiths, Wilmington's religious buildings present a wealth of outstanding architectural statements. Beyond that, they show an astounding range of major trends in ecclesiastical building styles. From Federal style churches through Greek Revival, Gothic Revival, Moorish Revival, and Romanesque edifices to Neoclassical and Contemporary constructions, Wilmington has, or has had, them all.

The roster of nationally known architects commissioned to design these houses of worship is impressive. Likewise, skilled local architects and artisans have made important contributions to the contours of the religious cityscape. Hardly a stagnant backwater in the quality of its architectural expression, Wilmington possesses a record of religious architecture of great beauty comparable to the best religious architecture available in the state.

If religious architecture is about buildings, it is also about people and their faiths. For if architecture can and should be esteemed as an artistic statement in its own right, contextual understanding of congregations and their religious traditions deepens this appreciation. Wilmington, always more urban in tone and manner than the surrounding area, was until 1910 the state's largest city. As a seaport dating back to the eighteenth century, Wilmington has been the entry point for waves of immigrants. Some of these immigrants passed through on their way elsewhere, but many stayed, either in Wilmington or in the Cape Fear region. With these immigrants came their religions: English Anglicans, French Huguenots, Scottish and Welsh Calvinists, German Lutherans, Irish Catholics, Polish Jews, Greek Orthodox Christians and, more recently, Thai Buddhists and Pakistani Muslims, all have helped to make up the diverse religious landscape that is Wilmington past and present.

Clearly the history of religion in Wilmington is more than just theology; it includes ethnicity, class, gender, prelates, pastors, and people in the pews. This essay, and the text and images that make up the accompanying exhibit, cannot delve into all these aspects. Nor do the exhibit and the essay provide a complete inventory of all the religious buildings or of their congregations in Wilmington. Instead, they seek to illustrate the depth and richness of the architectural legacy of religious buildings in historic Wilmington.

During the colonial era, the Anglican congregation of St. James was the first formally organized church in Wilmington. Yet there were Methodist, Presbyterian, and Baptist preachers in eighteenth-century Wilmington; a Jewish family lived here, too. The 1850s were expansive days in Wilmington. With the completion of the Wilmington and Weldon railroad, Wilmington's economy improved and the city's population grew. Thomas Fanning Wood, a local physician, sketched a social portrait of several antebellum congregations, noting that the town's mercantile element dominated among the Presbyterians, while the Methodists "were foremost in their attention to the needs of public worship among the slaves." The Methodist church, he continued, "was an inviting house to the masses of the population who found the seats free, the worship simple." On the eve of the Civil War, Wood identified a spectrum of churches in Wilmington including the Presbyterian, Methodist, Episcopal, Catholic, Baptist, and Lutheran.

After the Civil War, the religious landscape blossomed with the organization of several black churches. While some blacks remained in the churches which they had attended prior to the War, many left to form new congregations. Black Baptist, Presbyterian, and Episcopal churches were formed; new congregations of the African Methodist Episcopal and African Methodist Episcopal Zion faiths were organized as well. In the late nineteenth and early twentieth centuries black Baptist, A.M.E., and A.M.E. Zion denominations grew and new independent religious traditions also appeared in the African American community.

The first third of the twentieth century found some congregations moving to and others beginning in the newly developed suburbs. By this time Roman Catholic and Jewish communities had visually reaffirmed their identities with stunning new buildings, while many downtown Protestant congregations rebuilt or added to their established church structures.

Reflecting national trends, religious diversity in Wilmington increased by the mid-twentieth century. A Russian Orthodox church began in 1932 in Burgaw and a Greek Orthodox congregation was incorporated in Wilmington in 1943. An Islamic congregation has existed in Wilmington since 1973, and a Theravada Buddhist community in nearby Bolivia was established in 1988. Beyond that, other religious associations, some of which have existed for years in the Wilmington area, include the Society of Friends, the Unitarian Universalists, the Church of Jesus Christ of Latter-Day Saints, the Moravians, the Jehovah's Witnesses, the Salvation Army, the Pentecostals, the Bahai's, the Metropolitan Community Church, the Adventists, the Christian Scientists, the Assemblies of God, and a variety of nondenominational organizations.

Religious life in Wilmington has been complex, diverse, and reflective of its people's challenges and hopes. Sacred spaces, whether seen in soaring steeples, church graveyards, or natural areas hallowed by tradition or function, give visibility to that life and allow it to become tangible, public, and dynamic expressions which all can experience and appreciate.

Dr. Walter H. Conser, Jr. is a professor of religious studies and professor of historyat the University of North Carolina at Wilmington.

HISTORIC WILMINGTON CHURCHES

Edward F. Turberg

The numerous churches that scatter through Wilmington's historic district and suburban reaches are significant expressions of the advanced architectural tastes of past generations as well as being, in many cases, forerunners of national styles later embraced by other cities in the country. Dating from the mid-eighteenth to the early twentieth centuries, these religious institutions form the fabric of the cultural community.

Sacred Spaces: Architecture and Religion in Historic Wilmington samples the spectrum of Wilmington's ecclesiastical architecture from the vernacular to the high-style. Viewed by the architectural historian, a select, extant collection of these houses of worship underscores Wilmington's historic commitment to excellence in the design of religious structures.

St. James Episcopal Church is the nucleus of one of the earliest religious institutions in the Cape Fear region. The rector and vestry of St. James chose to build a new edifice in 1839. In the new St. James, Philadelphia architect Thomas Ustick Walter produced a landmark of picturesque architecture—the first full-fledged example of Gothic Revival in the South, and one of the first in the nation.

In 1845, the Roman Catholic congregation asked the builders of St. James Church, J.C. and R.B. Wood, to design them a house of worship in a similar style. The result was St. Thomas the Apostle Church on Dock Street, dedicated in 1847. Lacking a central tower, the facade is highlighted by a triple lancet arch above the entrance. The brick exterior was stuccoed in 1858.

Chestnut Street Presbyterian Church, initially Second Presbyterian Church, is a rare frame structure sheathed with board-and-batten "Carpenter Gothic" walls which incorporate paired-arch Italianate windows—a unique example, perhaps, of "Carpenter Italianate."

Two antebellum examples of Wilmington's ecclesiastical architecture, First Presbyterian and First Baptist, were entrusted to another Philadelphia architect, Samuel Sloan. His past work embraced Greek and Gothic Revival as well as Romanesque and Italianate styles. Both begun in 1859, the two churches differed in plans, the Presbyterians using a traditional long nave, while the Baptists adopted a broader auditorium plan. When completed, the 197-foot high spire of the Baptist Church was said to be the tallest steeple in America.

Another antebellum construction was St. Paul's Lutheran Church on Market Street in the then-suburban section of Wilmington. Created by local architect H. Vollers and executed by James F. Post, St. Paul's wide, pointed-arch windows contain the most elegant stained glass windows in the entire region, rich representations of the finest glazier's art of the early twentieth century.

Post-Civil War Wilmington ushered in an era of accelerated activity in church construction in the Cape Fear. Of particular importance was the establishment of black congregations throughout the port city. St. Mark's Episcopal Church was a rare southern design by Boston architect

William Ralph Emerson, who specialized in building pretentious summer homes for wealthy clients in coastal New England. Emerson copied rural English Gothic forms in the low eaves, high ridge, and octagonal corner tower.

St. Stephen's A.M.E. Church was designed in 1880 by Lewis Hollingsworth, a member of the congregation. Construction was performed by other members who were skilled brick masons, carpenters and artisans. The construction, completed in 1888, became a north side landmark of late Gothic Revival design.

Fifth Avenue Methodist Church was built the year following St. Stephen's and the congregation turned to yet another Philadelphia architect, B. D. Price, to design their sanctuary. The projecting facade is enriched by triple lancets, surmounted by a circular window containing a six-pointed star, and a stepped brick pattern in the roof slopes.

The antebellum First Presbyterian Church was devastated by fire on New Year's Eve 1925. For the new church, New York architect Hobart Upjohn created a distinguished French Gothic conception of urban scale composed of rugged granite that rises to the very peak of the steeple above a sturdy stone tower.

Two Wilmington houses of worship inspire Mediterranean rather than Northern European associations in their form and detail. The first, St. Mary Roman Catholic Church, is a careful rendering of Spanish Baroque architecture designed and built by Rafael Guastavino and his son Rafael Jr. The second structure is the Temple of Israel, built in 1875 for the first Reformed Jewish congregation in the state. Moorish arches and gilded domes atop the corner towers stress the Sephardic roots of the sect and the expanding use of the style in European and American synagogues.

Suburban churches were built in communities that developed along the streetcar lines. Especially important are three religious structures skirting Market Street in Carolina Heights. The first two are Gothic in inspiration: St. Andrews-Covenant Presbyterian Church (1917), by Kenneth Murchison of New York and James F. Gause of Wilmington; and St. Paul's Episcopal Church (1956-58), by Lynch and Foard, Wilmington architects who produced many of the neighborhood's residences. The Neoclassical Revival Trinity Methodist (1920), by Leslie N. Boney for W.J. Wilkins & Company of Wilmington, stands adjacent to New Hanover High School, which the firm also designed in 1919-25.

Twentieth century churches continue to rise throughout the Cape Fear region and are immediately recognizable for their stylistic associations with national tastes and styles. The tent-like designs of the First Christian Church and Pine Valley Methodist Church, together with the contemporary flair of St. Mark's Roman Catholic Church are exemplary of the fact that Wilmington retains its distinction as a national forerunner in inspirational religious architecture.

"Not Even in New York"

Tony Wrenn, Hon. AIA, CA
Fredericksburg, Virginia

Some years ago I gave a slide lecture in Wilmington titled "Not Even in New York." The talk was about Wilmington's architecture, and I noted that from one street corner in Wilmington, Third at Market, I believed one could see works by more nationally known architects than one could see from any street corner in New York City. Samuel Sloan, Thomas U. Walter, Henry Dudley, John Norris, Carrere and Hastings, Hobart Upjohn, James A Wetmore, John M. Trimble, R. Stanley Brown, local boys Henry Bacon and Kenneth M. Murchison, and others had perfectly preserved works in plain view from that street corner.

In the hundred years between the 1830s and the 1930s Wilmington, with a population that did not reach 10,000 until 1860, or 30,000 until the late 1930s, had a view of its own importance that led it to look toward such architects when it built. As North Carolina's major port, its citizens were well aware of the architectural masterpieces of other areas and of the architects who produced them. Even as Wilmingtonians traveled and looked outward, the area produced home town architects of great competency and capability, and employed them in design as well.

It was public buildings that outsiders came to town to design, and many of those were churches. Within a few blocks of Walter's, Upjohn's and Sloan's sanctuaries, stand churches by Rafael Guastavino, William Ralph Emerson and Harold E. Wagoner.

Fine interiors, great organs, and superb stained glass completed the works of these master architects. The congregants who commissioned these designs and had them constructed, said to all "look at what this congregation is capable of, and look at the pride we take in it." And they said as well, "look at me and learn how I feel about myself, my religion, and my town."

There may be other cities and towns that equal Wilmington in its devotion to God, and the capability to express devotion in buildings, but I know of no other American city of Wilmington's size that can equal it, nor do I know of any other city of its size where so many significant works exist in such a small downtown area. That so many of Wilmington's churches exist in settings of historic streets, and preserved buildings and landscapes, gives the area's sacred spaces extra value.

What a great deal there is to view, to savor and to learn from these spaces. I applaud Preservation North Carolina, The Bellamy Mansion, and all associated with this exhibition for making the experience possible. But most of all, I applaud the citizens of the Wilmington area for providing us with, and for preserving, such a spectacular heritage.

Amon Carter Museum, Fort Worth, Texas

St. James Episcopal Church
Unknown photographer,
daguerreotype, c. 1847.
P1981.65.28

Believed to be the earliest outdoor photograph in North Carolina.

Director's Acknowledgments

Jonathan Noffke

Sacred Spaces: Architecture and Religion in Historic Wilmington is an ambitious exhibition and publishing project for the Bellamy Mansion Museum. It draws upon dozens of historical and architectural resources to tell the story of how religion and buildings have shaped Wilmington, North Carolina's development.

To say that Wilmington has a rich collection of historic religious architecture is a vast understatement. Others have attested to the significance of the Port City's architectural heritage in the preceding catalog essays. What often goes unsaid in the discussion of Wilmington's celebrated architecture is that we enjoy the benefit of so many talented and generous people, past and present, who have recorded and shared their knowledge and interest in the subject of history. Wilmington is doubly blessed with a long and fascinating past and an extensive group of researchers and historians who continue to bring that history to life.

I want to extend a special thanks to guest curator, Dr. Walt Conser. His generosity of time and his vast knowledge of the subject have made this a quality project and one that is a pleasure to produce. His willingness to devote a semester of research and effort to this endeavor is a great gift to our institution. We gratefully acknowledge the trio of Beverly Tetterton, Ed Turberg, and Janet Seapker. Each has been a phone call away to advise, edit, answer questions, and share their encyclopedic knowledge of Wilmington history. The research of Tony Wrenn and Bill Reaves has been a tremendous resource, as well as various works by Susan Block, Anne Russell, Diane Cashman, Catherine Bishir, Vera Brunges, Gibbs Willard, Anne Hutteman, and Steve McAllister. Thank you Joe Sheppard, Tim Bottoms, Jerry Cotten and Steve Massengill for your helpfulness in securing images. Thanks to volunteers Bill Boney, Paul Bowerman, Margaret Hutchins, David Jones, Lydia McCormack, Clif Montford and Tim Stoltz for lending a hand with the exhibition production. The contribution of UNCW interns Blair Jackson for her tireless work on this project and that of Kristen Ostiguy in gathering images has been invaluable to the process. Thanks to Tony Janson, Tom Macie and Kemille Moore from the UNCW Art and Theatre Department for their cooperation. We also wish to thank catalog designer Julie Macie and editorial assistants Suzanne Roth and Maggie Noffke for their work on this project. Additional credit should be extended to the dozens of churches and archival repositories who have loaned images and information to make *Sacred Spaces* possible.

Tabitha McEachern is great friend to the Bellamy Mansion and Wilmington's cultural life. Her support is very special to us. She consistently amazes us with acts of great generosity to support worthwhile projects. Thank you, Tabitha. We also gratefully acknowledge the additional support of the Landfall Foundation and Atlantic Printing.

EIGHTEENTH-CENTURY BEGINNINGS

Not long after Wilmington was established in the early 1700s, the colonial legislature organized a parish.

St. James Episcopal's congregation completed their first church in 1770. By 1826, three other denominations had established congregations in Wilmington.

George Whitefield, a friend of John Wesley, visited the Cape Fear region in 1739 and preached in Wilmington in 1747. In 1797, William Meredith, a Wesleyan missionary, settled in Wilmington and started its first Methodist church. Early Methodism was noteworthy for predominantly black congregations. Francis Asbury, the "father of American Methodism," visited Wilmington in 1803 and noted that the Methodist congregation had "eight hundred and seventy eight Africans and a few whites."

Although there was a Baptist presence in the area as early as 1766, it was 1808 before the first Baptist association was formed in Wilmington. By 1826 Baptists had constructed a two-story meetinghouse on Front Street.

Though Presbyterian minister Hugh McAden had preached in Wilmington in 1756, the earliest Presbyterian church was not constructed until 1819. This building burned down the same year and was rebuilt in 1821 on the same Front Street location, in a Federal style with a steeple and two-story portico.

OLD PRESBYTERIAN CHURCH, WILMINGTON, N. C.

The 1821 Federal Style First Presbyterian Church on Front Street replaced an earlier meetinghouse in the same location. James Marshall and Benjamin Jacobs are credited as the builders. The church served the congregation until it was razed by fire in 1859.

FIRST PRESBYTERIAN CHURCH

Below: The earliest church in the region was St. Phillip's Anglican at the colonial settlement at Brunswick Town. The church was built in 1751 and was burned during the American Revolution. This photograph shows visitors to the St. Phillip's ruins just after the turn of the century.

McALLISTER & SOLOMON USED AND RARE BOOKS

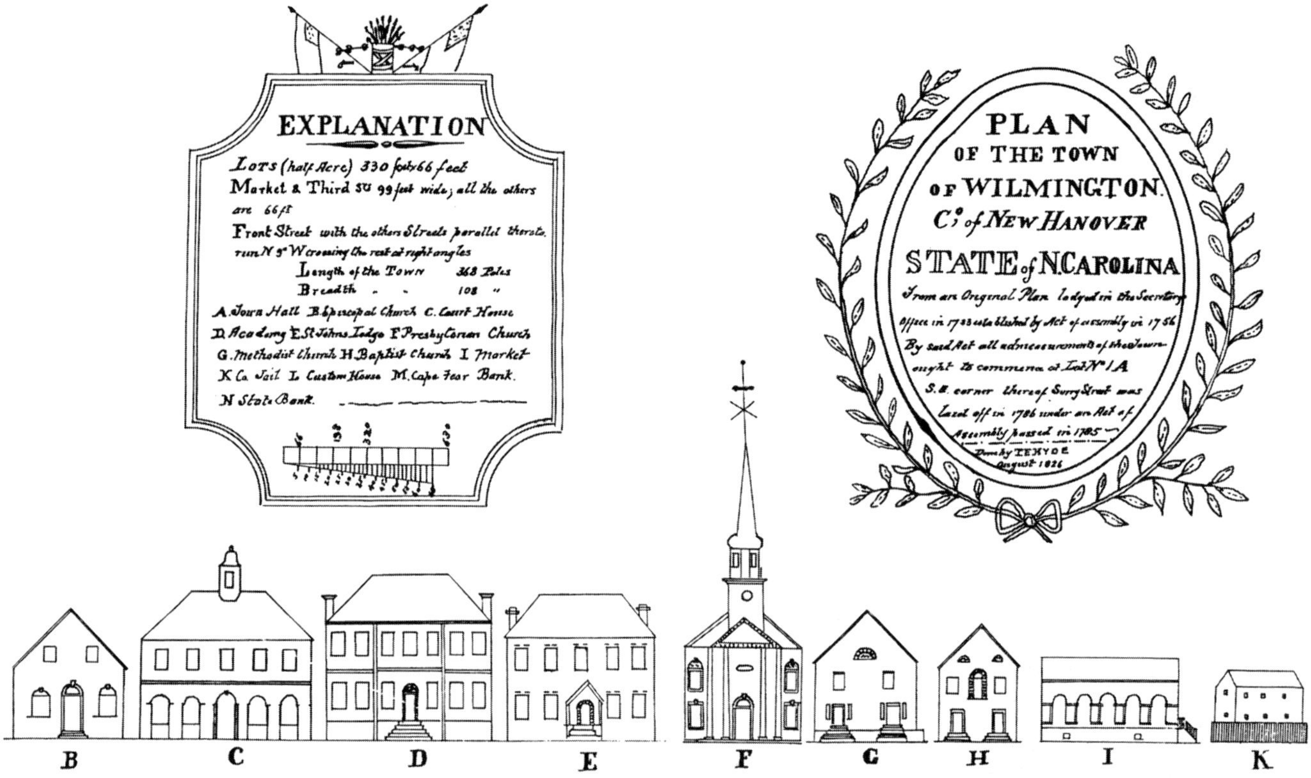

The 1826 Hyde Map of Wilmington shows a number of the young city's more notable structures. These illustrations, excerpted from the map, include four early churches: The Episcopal Church (B), located on Market Street between Third and Fourth; The Presbyterian Church (F) on Front Street, between Dock and Orange; The Methodist Church (G) near the corner of Front and Walnut Streets; The Baptist Church (H) on Front Street between Ann and Nun. This last location is still known as Baptist Hill.

NHCPL, LOCAL HISTORY ROOM

Religious Growth and Architectural Refinement

By the 1830s and 1840s, religious architecture reached a greater level of sophistication as congregations constructed new and more elaborate churches. Mt. Lebanon Chapel, dating to 1835, was built near Bradley Creek as a summer chapel for St. James Episcopal. The St. James congregation demolished their old church in 1839 and chose Thomas U. Walter to design a new structure at Third and Market Streets. Walter's precedent-setting design was one of America's first uses of the Gothic Revival style in ecclesiastical architecture. Reminiscent of St. Luke's at Chelsea, with its crenellated battlements and lancet windows, the new St. James structure architecturally personified the church's battle against evil.

In 1821, Bishop John England found 22 Roman Catholics in Wilmington; by 1845 and the appointment of Father

The 1835 Mt. Lebanon Chapel is the oldest standing church in New Hanover County. It is located near Bradley Creek in Airlie Gardens.

CFM Image Archives: Wilmington Star News

Thomas Murphy to Wilmington, the number had grown to 40. The same year, St. Thomas the Apostle Roman Catholic Church was constructed and drew on St. James's for its architectural vocabulary of windows and roof design in the Gothic style.

One of Wilmington's finest examples of the Greek Revival style in religious architecture was Front Street Methodist Church. This, the third church in the congregation's history, was built in 1844. With massive Doric columns and pedimented portico, the building epitomized classical proportion and simplicity.

Front Street Methodist Church constructed its impressive new Greek Revival structure in 1844. The cupola was added in the second decade after the initial construction. This building (the congregation's third) was destroyed by fire in 1886.

GRACE STREET METHODIST CHURCH

In 1845, Wilmington's small Roman Catholic congregation constructed a new church, St. Thomas the Apostle, on Dock Street, between Second and Third. The design for the building borrowed from the Gothic form of St. James.

ST. MARY'S ROMAN CATHOLIC CHURCH

St. James Episcopal Church (shown at left in 1873) began construction of a new church in 1839 to replace a smaller meetinghouse located on the same property on Market Street, between Third and Fourth Streets. Thomas U. Walter's stylish Gothic Revival design set a new architectural standard for Wilmington churches.

NC COLLECTION, UNC LIBRARY AT CHAPEL HILL

Antebellum Wilmington

From the 1820s onward, a growing number of church steeples punctuated the Wilmington skyline. Commerce had increased dramatically by the 1850s, and the riverfront bustled as improved river and rail systems linked the hinterlands to Wilmington and Wilmington to the world. By 1850, the city's population grew to 7,264, of whom 3,031 were slaves and 652 were free blacks. There were six churches in town and several new congregations would soon begin.

Like people in other antebellum cities, Wilmingtonians participated in several reform movements. Educational and cultural opportunities developed slowly in North Carolina, but organizations emerged to fill a variety of community needs. During the antebellum era, the education of poor female children and aid to the destitute was undertaken in the city by organizations such as the Ladies Benevolent Society. The North Carolina Bible Society, a group organized to distribute bibles, became active locally. The North Carolina Temperance Society, organized in 1831, was also operating in Wilmington. As a port city with sailors disembarking and waiting to ship out again, a Seamen's Friend Society began in 1835 "to improve the social, moral, and religious condition of seamen." In 1859 the Seamen's Bethel opened; it provided a boardinghouse, which the Society hoped would guard the sailors against what it called "the insidious snares and seductive vices" with which the city tempted them.

Antebellum Wilmington enjoyed a booming economy, most of it driven by the busy port, the area's natural resources, banking, and rail connections. By 1860 Wilmington was home to nearly 10,000 residents. It was North Carolina's largest city.

BELLAMY MANSION MUSEUM COLLECTION

Seamen's Bethel was an outgrowth of one of several reform movements popular in antebellum Wilmington. The Seamen's Friend Society dedicated this structure at the corner of Front and Dock Streets in 1859. Each Sunday afternoon, a local minister conducted services for sailors who were in port.

NHCPL Local History Room

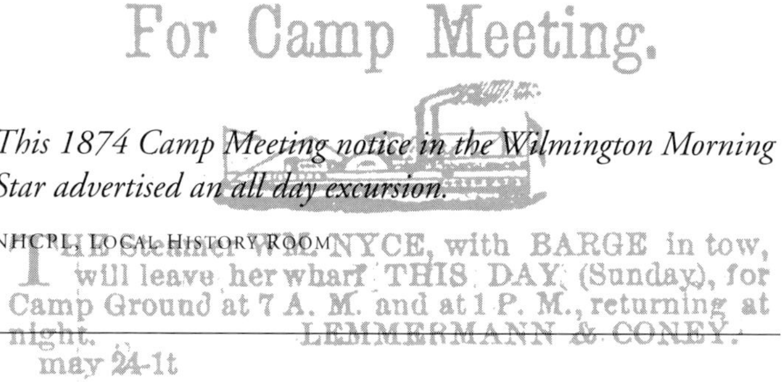
For Camp Meeting.

THE Steamer WM. NYCE, with BARGE in tow, will leave her wharf THIS DAY (Sunday), for Camp Ground at 7 A. M. and at 1 P. M., returning at night. LEMMERMANN & CONEY.

may 24-1t

This 1874 Camp Meeting notice in the Wilmington Morning Star advertised an all day excursion.

NHCPL Local History Room

The Revival of 1858

While revivals, quarterly meetings, camp meetings, communion seasons, and mission campaigns had all occurred before and came after, the Revival of 1858 was distinctly different. Largely a national urban movement with beginnings in New York City, this revival was organized around interdenominational midday prayer meetings led by businessmen. In part a response to the economic panic of 1857 and in part to the sectional, political, and denominational divisions of the day, the Revival of 1858 emphasized unity, avoided controversial topics, and encouraged domestic missions. Some local congregations grew in numbers, undertook new projects, or began missionary ventures from the enthusiasm generated by the revival. The local chapter of the YMCA, one of the first in the state, got its start from the revival's spiritual and organizational impulses.

This wave of self-improvement and moral awareness gave birth to a significant period of church construction in Wilmington.

The Young Men's Christian Association (YMCA) had its beginnings in the Revival of 1858. The local organization started in antebellum Wilmington, but the effort was cut short by the Civil War. The local movement began anew later in the nineteenth century and the YMCA built its new Wilmington headquarters (shown here) in 1891 at the corner of Front and Grace Streets. A new headquarters was built in 1912 at the corner of Market and Third.

NHCPL Local History Room, Fales Collection.

Outdoor camp meetings, like this one in Macon County, were popular throughout the nineteenth and early twentieth century in North Carolina.

NC Collection, UNC Library at Chapel Hill

FRUITS OF THE SPIRIT

The Revival of 1858 influenced five notable examples of new church construction in Wilmington.

St. John's Episcopal Church at Third and Red Cross Streets began in 1853 as a missionary extension of St. James Episcopal. A new building was completed on the same site in 1860, in an English Gothic parish church style.

St. Paul's Episcopal, located initially at Fourth and Orange, was built under the auspices of Bishop Thomas Atkinson in 1858. The church, with free seating and a racially mixed congregation, closed in 1862 due to the yellow fever epidemic. It reopened in 1866 as a mission for blacks, many of whom left in 1869 to form their own congregation. St. Paul's moved to its present location at Market and Sixteenth Streets in 1914.

In 1858, fourteen members of First Presbyterian Church purchased a lot on Chestnut Street and commissioned the construction of the Second Presbyterian Church. Built by a Mr. Moody, the board-and-batten structure combined elements of the Carpenter Gothic and Italianate style. During the war years, these original members returned to the First Presbyterian Church; they sold the building to a group of black Presbyterians in October 1866. These individuals organized the First Colored Presbyterian Church in April 1867, later changing its name to the Chestnut Street Presbyterian Church. David Sadgwar, Alfred Hargrave, and Henry Taylor, all skilled black artisans in the city, were among the trustees of this congregation.

In 1858, Baptists, who had reorganized themselves in

St. John's Episcopal Church at Third and Red Cross Streets was completed in 1860. It replaced a small mission begun in 1853 on the same site. At the time of the church's construction, it was in one of Wilmington's prime residential areas. The congregation moved to a suburban Forest Hills location in 1955. The original church was later demolished.

NC COLLECTION, UNC LIBRARY AT CHAPEL HILL

1833 and had been worshipping together in a meetinghouse on Front Street, purchased a lot on the corner of Market and Fifth. They commissioned Philadelphia architect Samuel Sloan to design their new church. His plans called for an Early English Gothic structure with two soaring spires, a design suitably expressing the affluence of antebellum Wilmington. Construction began in 1859, but war and slow funding delayed completion until 1870.

Construction of St. Paul's Lutheran church also began in 1859. Mr. H. Vollers, a member of the congregation, submitted a design for a Gothic Revival structure with a pedimented facade and a spire topped central tower. Local contractor James F. Post, hired to supervise the construction, may have also had a hand in the design. Like First Baptist, the construction of St. Paul's was delayed by the Civil War and not completed until 1869.

Framed by a massive Gothic arch, First Baptist's chancel (shown here in the 1890's) housed both the choir loft and the organ's pipes. Note the elaborate hanging chandelier.

FIRST BAPTIST CHURCH

Like St. Paul's Lutheran, First Baptist Church began a construction project that was slowed by the Civil War. Philadelphia architect Samuel Sloan's Gothic-revival design featured two soaring spires; the taller of the pair reached 197 feet into the sky. At the time of its completion, according to local tradition, the church boasted the tallest steeple in America.

CFM IMAGE ARCHIVES

Below: While the church structure at Fourth and Orange was first occupied by Episcopalians in 1858, it appears that the parish purchased the structure from a Methodist congregation in order to establish free seating and interracial worship for the new St. Paul's congregation.

NHCPL LOCAL HISTORY ROOM

ST. PAUL'S EPISCOPAL.
Fourth and Orange Streets.

Above: Constructed in 1858 on Chestnut between Seventh and Eighth Streets as the Second Presbyterian Church, the structure changed hands in 1866 and became Chestnut Street Presbyterian Church. This early image shows the building's original open portico on the gable end. The portico was enclosed late in the nineteenth century.

FIRST PRESBYTERIAN CHURCH

Although construction began a decade earlier, St. Paul's Lutheran at Sixth and Market Streets was not completed until 1869. Members held services in the session room projecting from the rear of the sanctuary until completion. This 1873 image shows the building in its original exposed brick finish. A year later, the exterior was finished in stucco. A 1907-08 renovation under architect Henry Bonitz added transepts to the sanctuary and removed the session room.

NC Collection, UNC Library at Chapel Hill

Yellow Fever and War's Defeat

Above: Food was in short supply during the military occupation of Wilmington. This etching portrays Wilmingtonians standing in line for rations at the Union Commissary on Market Street in April 1865.

Cape Fear Museum

The "streets were empty, save the rolling sounds of hearses or physicians' vehicles. The dogs howled from hunger, and the very birds of the air had deserted the city. Death and pestilence had possession of every place."

— *Newspaper description of Wilmington during the Yellow Fever Epidemic*

The exact number of casualties is not known, but thousands were afflicted and hundreds perished in Wilmington during an 1862 yellow fever epidemic. Some churches closed their doors and all struggled to minister to the ill, as members died and others fled the city. Robert Drane, rector of St. James Episcopal; John Pritchard, pastor of First Baptist; and Thomas Murphy, priest at St. Thomas the Apostle, all remained to assist the sick. Each fell victim to the disease.

In the aftermath of Wilmington's fall to Federal troops in February 1865, some congregations suffered under the military occupation. Alfred Watson, rector of St. James, continued to offer prayers for the Confederate government. Upon learning this, the Union commander, General Joseph R. Hawley, retaliated by seizing the church and converting it into a military hospital, tearing out the pews and furnishings. St. Paul's Lutheran's unfinished church was occupied by Federal soldiers who camped in the churchyard and used pews and desks for fuel, while stabling horses in the church. Other congregations lost items to looters. The Pulpit Bible of First Presbyterian, stolen by a Union soldier, ironically, was saved from a later fire. It was returned safely to the congregation in 1928.

Right: Union military officials enlisted the aid of freedmen to help remedy the deplorable sanitation conditions in wartime Wilmington.

CAPE FEAR MUSEUM

THE WILMINGTON "SANITARY COMMISSION"—CONTRABAND STREET-SWEEPERS GOING TO WORK.—FROM A SKETCH BY OUR SPECIAL ARTIST.

The wartime yellow fever epidemic had a devastating effect on Wilmington and the local clergy. (Left) Rev. Robert Brent Drane (St. James), (Center) Father Thomas Murphy (St. Thomas), and (Right) Rev. J.L. Pritchard (First Baptist) all died while ministering to the ill.

PHOTOGRAPHS COURTESY OF ST. JAMES EPISCOPAL, ST. MARY'S CATHOLIC, AND FIRST BAPTIST

Robert Drane

Thomas Murphy

John Pritchard

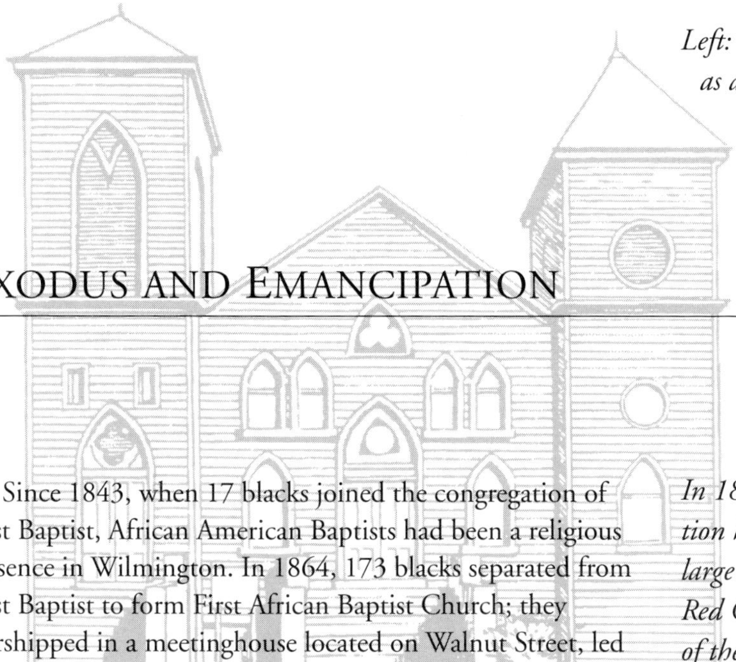

Left: The 1869 First African Baptist Church was constructed as a frame building. The facade was later clad in brick. The structure was destroyed by fire in 1974.

FIRST BAPTIST CHURCH

EXODUS AND EMANCIPATION

Since 1843, when 17 blacks joined the congregation of First Baptist, African American Baptists had been a religious presence in Wilmington. In 1864, 173 blacks separated from First Baptist to form First African Baptist Church; they worshipped in a meetinghouse located on Walnut Street, led by W. H. Banks. In 1869, a new church, located at Fifth and Campbell Streets, was completed, and the congregation deleted the word African from their name.

During the Federal military occupation of Wilmington in 1865, approximately 640 black members of Front Street Methodist Church left that congregation. Under the direction of W. H. Hunter, a former slave who became a Methodist army chaplain, the group formed St. Stephen's African Methodist Episcopal Church. The congregation met in a simple frame structure until a new church was constructed in 1888. Lewis Hollingsworth, a member of the congregation, designed the brick church in a Gothic style with a prominent gable and an imposing, spire-topped tower anchoring the corner. Church members, many of whom were carpenters, joined with Hollingsworth in constructing the building.

In 1880 the old frame church that the St. Stephen's congregation had used since 1867 was demolished to make way for a large new brick sanctuary (below) at the corner of Fifth and Red Cross Streets. Although services were held in various parts of the structure, the construction of the church was not completed until 1888. The spire and bell tower were completed in 1894.

CFM IMAGE ARCHIVE

Expansion Among Black Churches

Formed by an 1868 secession from First African Baptist Church and led by the Reverend W. H. Banks, Ebenezer Missionary Baptist Church first met in a frame building on the city's south side. James F. Post completed plans for a subsequent church on South Seventh Street between Orange and Ann Streets. This church was used from 1896 until 1927.

The American Missionary Association, a New England group which provided schools and churches to the newly freed slaves, donated the land for the Gregory Congregational Church building, which was completed in 1881. Its design was late Victorian Gothic with a single tower flanking the facade. The church was named for James J. Gregory of Marblehead, Massachusetts, who provided funds for the church and its adjacent school.

The nearby Christian Chapel, located on the corner of Seventh and Church Streets, later was renamed St. Luke's African Methodist Episcopal Zion. Bishop James W. Hood, who helped organize congregations in North Carolina after the Civil War, in fact, in 1865 brought the Christian Chapel congregation into the African Methodist Episcopal Zion denomination. A new church, designed in the prevailing Victorian Gothic style, was begun in 1878 and dedicated in 1882.

Organized first as a mission extension of St. Paul's Episcopal Church and separating from that group in 1869 to form their own congregation, St. Mark's Episcopal Church is the oldest Episcopal church built by and for a black congregation in North Carolina. Designed in Early English Gothic style by the Boston architects William Ralph Emerson and Carl Fehmer, the church has a steeply pitched roof and an octagonal tower. Constructed under the supervision of the Senior Warden Alfred Howe, an accomplished carpenter in his own right, the building was used first for worship in 1871 and consecrated in 1875.

The 1927 brick Ebenezer Baptist Church (shown here) was constructed near the site of the congregation's earlier sanctuary on South Seventh near Orange Street. Ebenezer Baptist has occupied a number of buildings since its formation in 1868. Their current house of worship is on Princess Place Drive.

CFM Image Archives

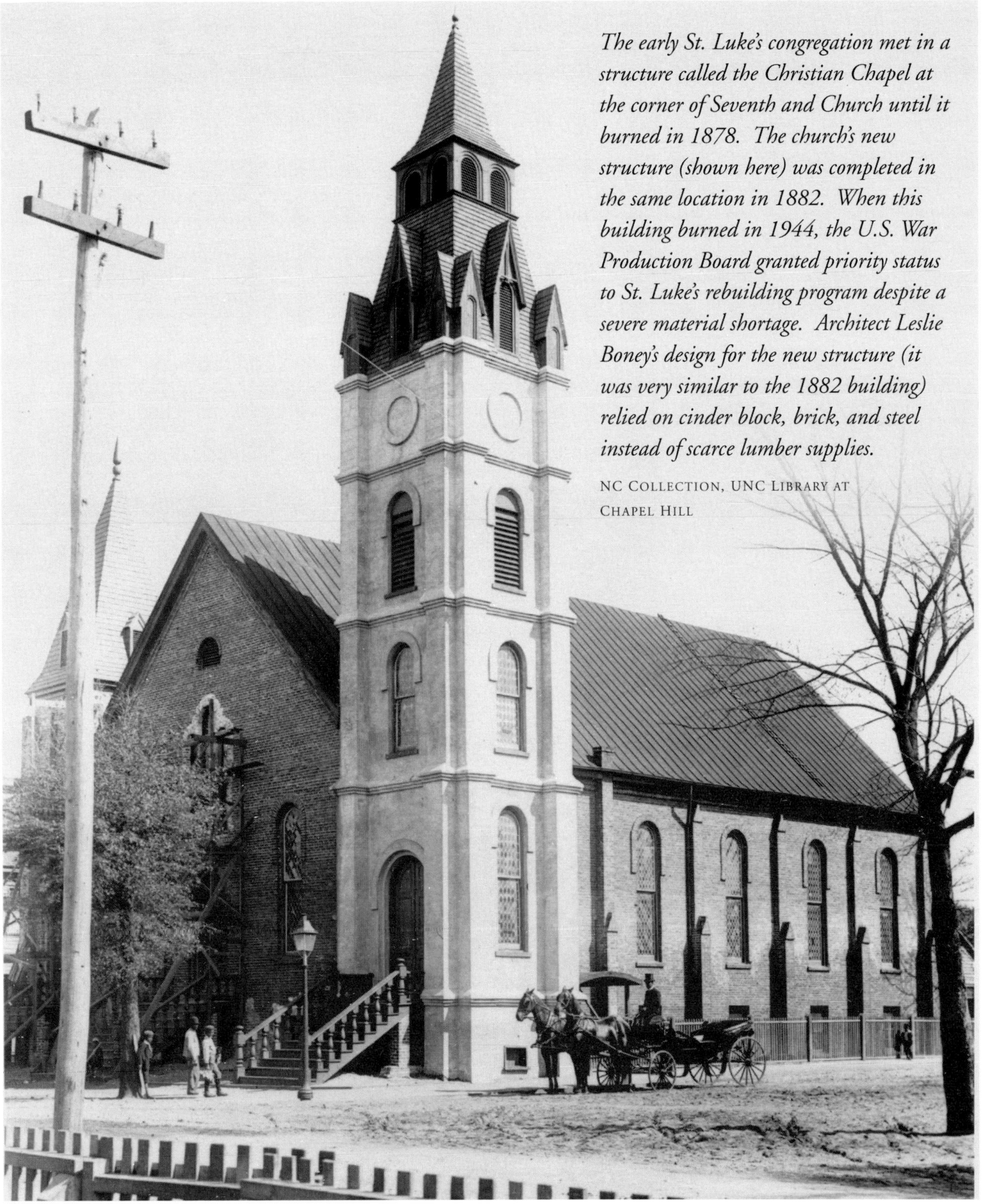

The early St. Luke's congregation met in a structure called the Christian Chapel at the corner of Seventh and Church until it burned in 1878. The church's new structure (shown here) was completed in the same location in 1882. When this building burned in 1944, the U.S. War Production Board granted priority status to St. Luke's rebuilding program despite a severe material shortage. Architect Leslie Boney's design for the new structure (it was very similar to the 1882 building) relied on cinder block, brick, and steel instead of scarce lumber supplies.

NC Collection, UNC Library at Chapel Hill

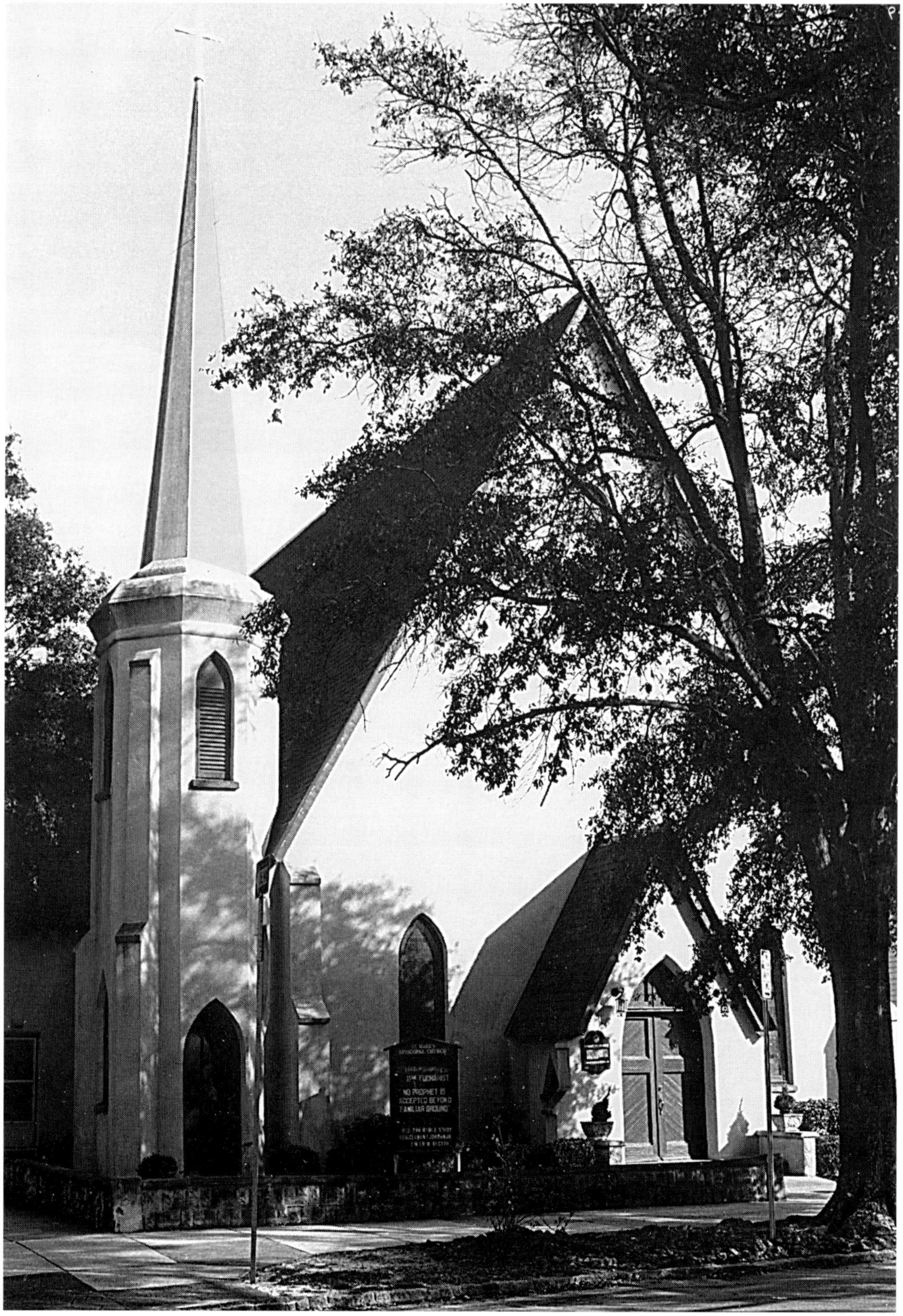

St. Mark's Episcopal formed their congregation in 1869 and by 1871 purchased a lot at the corner of Sixth and Mulberry (now Grace Street). In October, 1871, the ***Wilmington Star*** *reported that "St. Mark's Church rapidly approaches completion. The church building has been erected by the colored members of the Protestant Episcopal denomination in this city, and is one of the neatest edifices of its kind in the State."*

NHCPL Local History Room

Gregory Congregational Church began construction in 1880 on Nun Street, between Sixth and Seventh. By 1881, the 450 seat sanctuary, adorned with a 100 ft. steeple, was in use by the congregation. Unlike many early black Wilmington churches that had local origins, Gregory Congregational started as a northern mission. The church's bell is inscribed "The North to the South, in Sympathy and Love."

NHCPL LOCAL HISTORY ROOM

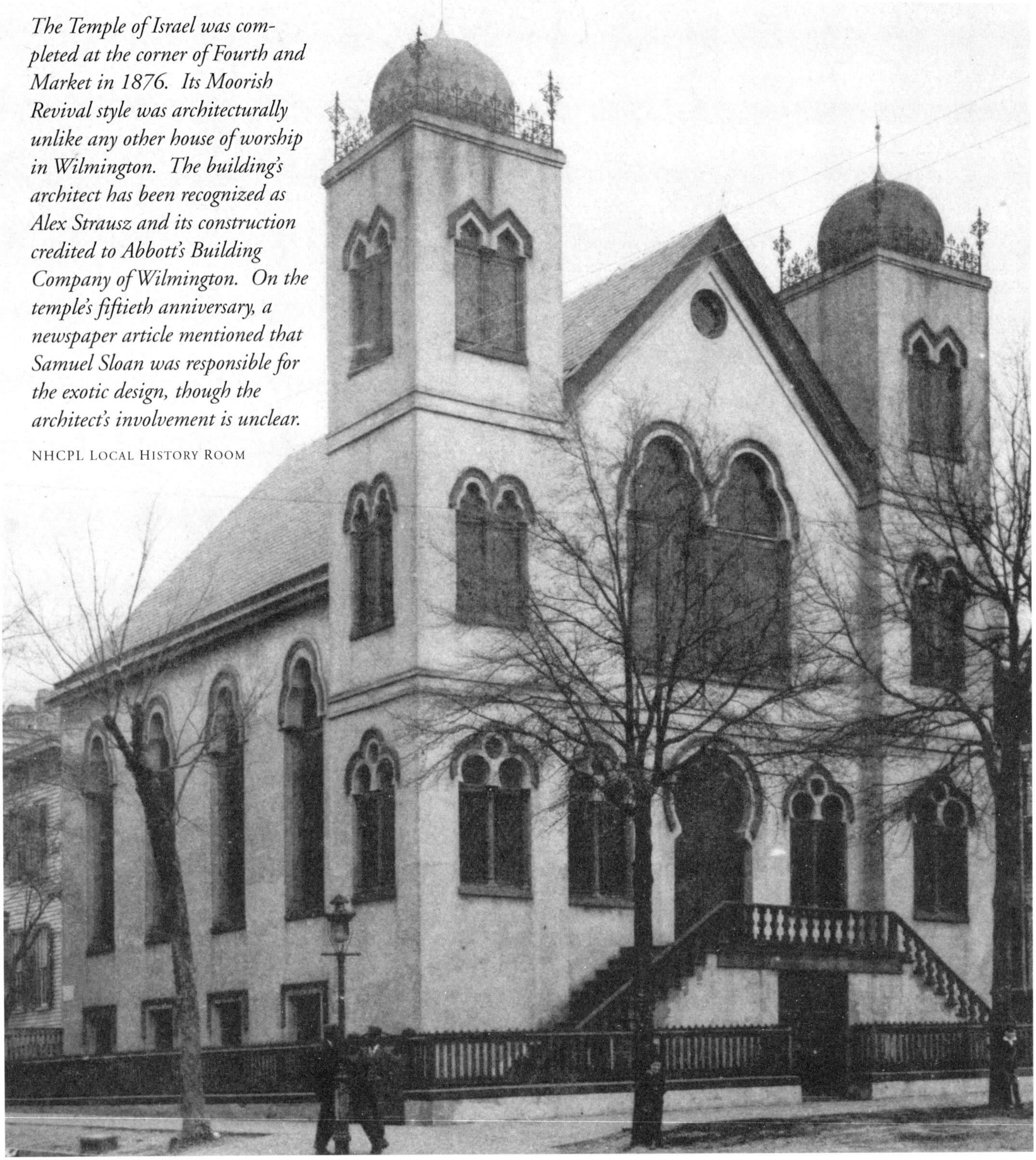

The Temple of Israel was completed at the corner of Fourth and Market in 1876. Its Moorish Revival style was architecturally unlike any other house of worship in Wilmington. The building's architect has been recognized as Alex Strausz and its construction credited to Abbott's Building Company of Wilmington. On the temple's fiftieth anniversary, a newspaper article mentioned that Samuel Sloan was responsible for the exotic design, though the architect's involvement is unclear.

NHCPL LOCAL HISTORY ROOM

Nineteenth Century Growth and Diversity

By 1882, more and more congregations dotted downtown Wilmington, as residential and commercial development extended the city's symbolic and spatial boundaries. This era saw an expansion of existing congregations and their facilities, as well as the construction of houses of worship for new populations.

Jews had lived in Wilmington since the early eighteenth century. While many of these early immigrants had come from Spain and Portugal, by the mid-1800s a new wave of Jewish immigrants, now from Germany, came to the United States, the South, and to Wilmington. Their temple, architecturally influenced by new synagogues in both Germany and elsewhere in the United States, was designed in the Moorish Revival style. Recent evidence suggests that Samuel Sloan might have played a role in developing the plans for the temple. The Temple of Israel, dedicated in 1876, houses the oldest continuous Jewish congregation in North Carolina. The German Jews generally reflected the Reform movement, which represented a revision of orthodox Judaism in the new context of America and modernity.

The construction of new churches predominated in late nineteenth century Wilmington, but they were not the only religious building programs. Well established churches such as St. James enlarged their facilities to meet the needs of growing memberships. A new St. James parish house (shown here) was completed in 1892. The structure faced Market Street behind the sanctuary. In preparation for the construction project, several graves were relocated to Oakdale Cemetery.

St. James Episcopal Church

PRESBYTERIAN AND METHODIST EXPANSION

The 1821 Federal style First Presbyterian Church burned in April 1859. Probably impressed with the plans taking shape at First Baptist, the Presbyterians commissioned Philadelphian Samuel Sloan to design, once again, a new Wilmington church. The result was a picturesque Gothic Revival edifice similar in many ways to the planned Baptist church. The Presbyterian house of worship was dedicated in its new location at Third and Orange Streets in April 1861.

In May 1873 the recently reactivated Second Presbyterian Church dedicated a new house of worship. In September 1888, the congregation changed its name to St. Andrew's Presbyterian, and in 1889 they completed a new church at Fourth and Campbell Streets. The new church was designed by Adolphus G. Bauer, who assisted Samuel Sloan in the design and construction of the governor's mansion in Raleigh.

Immanuel Chapel was organized originally as a mid-nineteenth century First Presbyterian mission. The congregation held services on Wooster Street until their move to a newly completed building on South Front Street in 1891. In 1921 the congregation moved to Fifth and Meares Streets and built a spacious Classical Revival style structure which they occupied until 1969.

Organized in 1847 and housed soon thereafter in a frame building, the congregation of Fifth Avenue Methodist Church dedicated a new church in 1890. Expressive of the High Victorian Gothic style with its pitched gable and

Rather than enlarge the 1873 Second Presbyterian sanctuary, the congregation (renamed St. Andrew's) decided to move forward with plans for a new church at the same location. The design (above) was furnished by architect Adolphus Gustavus Bauer. The brick Victorian Gothic St. Andrew's Presbyterian Church is Bauer's only identified project from his brief practice in Wilmington. The structure later served Holy Trinity Church and is currently being restored as a community art center.

NHCPL LOCAL HISTORY ROOM

flanked by two large towers, the building was designed by the Philadelphia architect, Benjamin D. Price. Price became the chief architect of the Methodist Church. He prepared annual catalogues distributed to churches in both the North and the South. He designed an auditorium-style sanctuary, a type popular in American Methodism until the 1920s. Additionally, Price created an Akron-style Sunday school – an assembly space adjacent to the sanctuary and separated by roll-up doors, which could be opened to extend sanctuary seating.

In 1873, the Second Presbyterian Church built a new brick sanctuary (above) near the corner of Fourth and Campbell. When the 1889 St. Andrew's sanctuary was completed, the old Second Presbyterian structure was incorporated into the rear of the new building.

FIRST PRESBYTERIAN CHURCH

The 1891 Immanuel Chapel on South Front Street (above) emerged from a mission formed earlier in the century. The congregation outgrew this building and constructed a new church at Fifth and Meares in 1921. The congregation disbanded in 1969.

FIRST PRESBYTERIAN CHURCH

Fifth Street Methodist was formed by Front Street Methodist church in 1847 to serve Wilmington's growing south side. In 1848, the simple frame structure (above) was completed in the 400 block of South Fifth Street. It served the congregation through the 1880's. Charlie Soong, a Chinese stowaway, was baptized in this building. After being educated in the United States he returned to his native China. One of his daughters became the wife of Chinese statesman Sun Yat-Sen, another daughter married Chinese President and Taiwanese leader Chiang Kai-Shek. T.V. Soong, one of his sons, became a prominent statesmen and financier in the Chinese government.

CFM IMAGE ARCHIVES

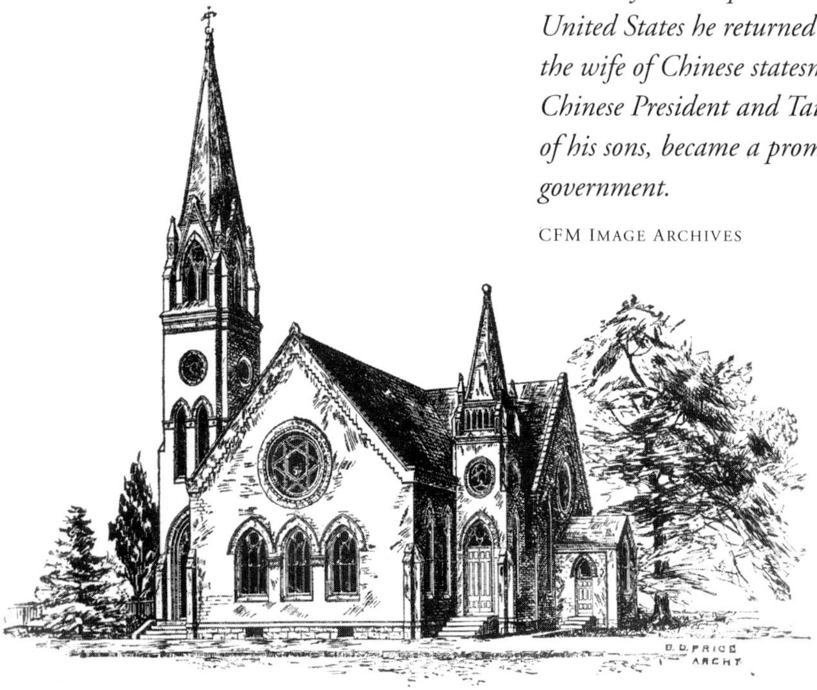

Architect B. D. Price of Philadelphia was responsible for the design (left) of Fifth Avenue Methodist's new Gothic church. His designs for Methodist churches were popular throughout the country. The spacious Fifth Avenue sanctuary seated 1,150 and was said to have held the state's largest capacity for a church when it was completed in 1890.

NC ARCHIVES AND HISTORY

Below: Rented pews and a substantial pipe organ were features of the 1861 First Presbyterian's interior.

First Presbyterian Church

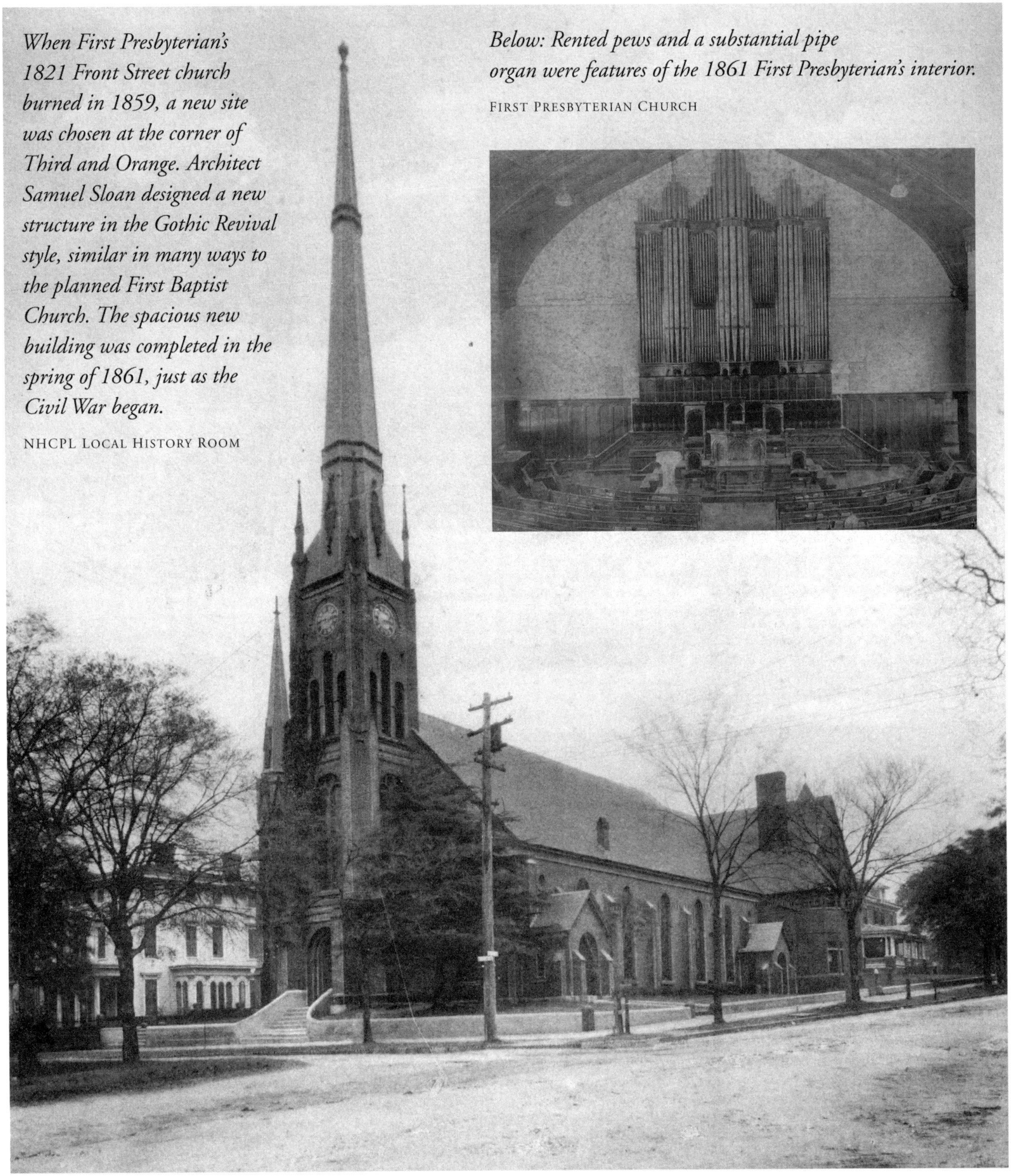

When First Presbyterian's 1821 Front Street church burned in 1859, a new site was chosen at the corner of Third and Orange. Architect Samuel Sloan designed a new structure in the Gothic Revival style, similar in many ways to the planned First Baptist Church. The spacious new building was completed in the spring of 1861, just as the Civil War began.

NHCPL Local History Room

Baptist and A.M.E. Expansion at the Turn of the Century

Central Baptist Church, located at Seventh and Red Cross Streets, had its beginnings in 1883 when the Reverend L.T. Christmas traveled to Wilmington to preach. After an 1887 fire destroyed this congregation's meetinghouse, they began construction on a Gothic Revival church with high pitched gables and arched stained glass windows. The building, substantially completed by1889, has been in continuous use since, making it the oldest black Baptist church building in the city.

Shiloh Baptist Church had its beginnings when a group left Ebenezer Baptist Church in 1883. The next year they dedicated their first church building at the corner of MacRae and Walnut Streets. In 1914 a new church in a Gothic Revival style with twin towers flanking the entrance was completed. The church burned in 1955 and was replaced.

Calvary Baptist originated in 1885 as a northside mission of First Baptist Church. The congregation met in a number of locations until the first building was completed in 1887 at the corner of Fourth and Brunswick. The congregation experienced steady growth and eventually sold their old structure. Calvary Baptist moved into their new church on 23rd Street in 1955.

The Southside Baptist congregation, organized in August 1894, worshipped in a frame structure at Fifth and Wooster. In 1913, the cornerstone was laid for a new church on the same site.

Calvary Baptist Church started as a small northside mission of First Baptist in 1886. They congregation grew rapidly and by 1906 they built a large new frame sanctuary at Fourth and Brunswick. In 1919 the church was veneered in brick. By 1938 the church had 1,350 members.

NHCPL Local History Room

Southside Baptist Church experienced rapid growth in the late nineteenth century. The new 1913 sanctuary at Fifth and Wooster (above) served the congregation until 1972.

NHCPL, Local History Room

Mt. Olive A.M.E.'s current church building (shown here) at Seventh and Wright was built in 1907. It replaced two earlier sanctuaries that were located near Second and Dawson.

NHCPL Local History Room

Mt. Zion A.M.E., originally located at Seventh and Howard, has occupied five buildings. Its 1873 building had to be rebuilt in 1882. That structure burned and its 1888 replacement was also destroyed by fire in 1900. In 1944, the turn-of-the-century sanctuary was condemned and a new building (shown left) was constructed at its present location at 1111 North Fifth.

NHCPL LOCAL HISTORY ROOM

Central Baptist Church (depicted here in an 1897 etching) began their building program in 1888 at Seventh and Red Cross Streets. Hurricane Hazel severely damaged the steeple in 1954 and it had to be removed.

NHCPL LOCAL HISTORY ROOM

Designed by J. M. McMichael of Charlotte, the new building had a pedimented porch and columns over a staired entrance. In 1972 the congregation moved to South College Road.

Located on Second Street between Dawson and Wright, Mt. Olive A.M.E. existed as early as the 1870s. A new church was completed in 1880. However, that building burned in 1907. The church's trustees purchased a lot on the corner of Seventh and Wright Streets to construct a new church.

The sister church, Mt. Zion A.M.E., also began in the 1870s and was located at North Seventh and Howard Streets. Between 1886 and 1900 this church was destroyed twice by fire. In September 1901, the Mt. Zion congregation laid the cornerstone for its new church. This church continued to be used until 1944, when the congregation moved to its newest site on North Fifth Street.

The
CHURCH
of
JESUS CHRIST
OF LATTER

New Times, New Beginnings

In 1886, the Greek Revival style Front Street Methodist Church burned and the congregation rebuilt on Mulberry at Fourth Street. The congregation chose to name itself Grace Methodist and dedicated its new building in December 1890. In 1895, the city renamed the street Grace Street, to honor the church. Here again, an auditorium style sanctuary adjoined the Akron-style Sunday school space, separated by roll-up doors, which could be used to extend or close off the worship area. This building was designed as a variation of the Romanesque style, a form immensely popular in both public and religious architecture in the late nineteenth and early twentieth centuries.

Begun in 1890 as a Sunday school located on North Fourth Street, St. Matthew's Lutheran Church was organized in March 1892. While St. Paul's Lutheran still used German in its services, St. Matthew's was designed as an English-speaking Lutheran congregation. The congregation built a new church on the corner of 17th and Ann Streets in 1942, after a fire had destroyed their old building. In 1972, the church moved again, this time to South College Road.

Mormon missionaries visited Wilmington as early as 1900. Their presence grew until a building committee was established and the Latter-Day Saints moved into their first chapel (left) in 1918. The members left this Castle Street location in 1949 when their new Borden Avenue church was completed.

Vera Brunges

The Christian Church (Disciples of Christ) first met in 1908 in a remodeled firehouse at the corner of Fourth and Dock Streets. By 1931 the congregation was meeting in the YMCA. They left downtown in 1963 and built a modern church structure on Oleander Drive.

The predecessor to the Episcopal Church of the Good Shepherd was a home for orphans and poor widows and later a chapel mission on the south side of Wilmington. Organized as a parish in 1907, a new church was constructed in 1911-12 on the corner of Queen and Sixth Streets, based on the plans drawn up by the then fledgling New York architects, Hobart Upjohn and George W. Conable. The building features a crenellated corner tower in the style of an English Gothic country church.

The Church of Jesus Christ of Latter-Day Saints, or Mormons, opened their first chapel in 1918 on Castle Street. Beginning in 1930, a second meetinghouse was begun at Market and Borden Streets; however, it was not dedicated until June 1950. The congregation (called a *ward* in the Mormon faith) is now in their third meetinghouse, this one on South College Road.

Above: St. Matthew's Lutheran started as a northside Sunday school at Fourth and Harnett. Their original English-speaking congregation met in this 1890s church. A fire later destroyed the structure.

McAllister & Solomon Used and Rare Books

When Front Street Methodist burned in 1886, the congregation chose a new location at Fourth and Mulberry to rebuild their new church (above). They renamed themselves Grace Methodist. In 1895 the city changed the street name from Mulberry to Grace. After a 1947 fire destroyed the church, nationally known architect Harold Wagoner of Philadelphia was commissioned to design a new house of worship.

NHCPL Local History Room

Wilmington's First Christian Church initially met in 1908 at a remodeled firehouse (right) near the corner of Fourth and Dock. They later moved to the YMCA and moved again in 1943 to a new structure (currently occupied by the Salvation Army) at Third and Ann.

FIRST CHRISTIAN CHURCH

Laying the cornerstone (below) for a church was generally accompanied by some type of commemoration. This photograph shows the November 1, 1911 Masonic ceremony performed at the Church of the Good Shepherd.

CHURCH OF THE GOOD SHEPHERD

Right: The 1912 Church of the Good Shepherd was the first of three Neo-Gothic designs for Wilmington church structures by New York architect Hobart Upjohn. After working as a engineer, Upjohn decided to pursue a career in architecture. The Church of the Good Shepherd at Sixth and Queen is the product of his six-year partnership with George Conable.

SHALL WE GATHER....

Well before the sacrament of baptism was performed inside the walls of a church, it was performed in rivers and lakes. Throughout the nineteenth and early twentieth centuries, the Cape Fear River and Wilmington's Greenfield Lake (shown here) were the scenes of numerous baptisms.

NHCPL LOCAL HISTORY ROOM, LOUIS T. MOORE COLLECTION

The concept of sacred spaces is not limited to the four walls of a church or a synagogue. From ancient times, people of widely varied faiths and beliefs have met in natural settings for worship and ritual expression. Whether by sprinkling or full immersion, Christian baptism is a ritual of initiation and symbolic of spiritual cleansing.

Funerary rituals are a significant rite of passage whether taking place in churchyards or public burial grounds and whether adorned with shells, stones, or marble slabs. Cemeteries, especially the rural and suburban variety, became popular in America in the mid-nineteenth century. Wilmington's Oakdale Cemetery was chartered in 1852 and patterned after the Mt. Auburn rural cemetery in Cambridge, Massachusetts. The wide paths and pleasant vistas of its spacious landscape encouraged visitors to enjoy its garden-like atmosphere. Its bucolic naturalism symbolized a space of restful sleep for those who had passed on. Sections, including the Hebrew Cemetery, the common grave of the victims of the 1862 Yellow Fever Epidemic, and the Memorial to the Confederate Dead, were later developed.

Above: Shortly after the original Oakdale Lodge burned in 1896, it was replaced with a larger version constructed of stone. Wilmington Architect James F. Post designed the 49 ft. x 36 ft., two-story structure. The brownstone building boasted men's and ladies' toilet rooms, a large reception room and the superintendents office.

NHCPL Local History Room

Oakdale Cemetery's landscaped setting included the Lodge completed in 1871, near the original entrance on the west side. Its Carpenter-Gothic design incorporated board-and-batten siding, scrolled barge boards and extensive lattice work. The building (seen at right around 1880) served as a chapel for burial services until it was destroyed by an 1896 stove fire. Note the extensive plantings and wide pathways.

NHCPL Local History Room

While nineteenth century African American cemeteries, like Wilmington's Pine Forest, did not have high-style statuary or landscaping, they often had burial sites heavily decorated with grave goods.

Bellamy Mansion Museum Collection

DOWNTOWN CHURCHES AND SYNAGOGUES

The early 20th century found church construction moving away from downtown Wilmington. Yet in an era of suburbanization and decentralization, some congregations bucked the trend and built or rebuilt in the central downtown area.

Construction of St. Mary's Roman Catholic Church began in 1908. The church was consecrated in 1912 and served as a Pro-Cathedral (the temporary seat of the bishop) until 1924. At that time, the diocese was established in Raleigh and the former Pro-Cathedral became St. Mary's Church. Rafael Guastavino and his son, Rafael, Jr., were responsible for the construction of this Spanish Baroque building with its twin towers and domed roof. Modeled in part on St. Lawrence Catholic Church, which the Guastavinos built in Asheville, North Carolina, St. Mary's is

This early interior photograph of St. Mary's shows its rich decoration of mosaics, statuary, and stained glass. The altar is the spatial centerpiece and focus of a Catholic church's interior.

ST. MARY'S ROMAN CATHOLIC CHURCH

Left: The successful design/construction team of Rafael Guastavino, Sr., and his son, Rafael, Jr., made a significant contribution to Wilmington architecture with their work on St. Mary's Roman Catholic Church. It was completed in 1911 at the corner of Fifth and Ann. The Spanish Baroque design employed a patented architectural brick-and-tile vault system pioneered by the Guastavinos. The father and son frequently stepped away from the role of designer and served as advisors and builders for some of America's most noted architects.

NHCPL LOCAL HISTORY ROOM

constructed of brick, terra cotta, and tiles, without the use of steel, wood, or nails. At first the parish was segregated with blacks worshipping at St. Thomas's and whites at St. Mary's. A 1966 fire closed St. Thomas and the parish was reunited in St. Mary's Church.

In the 1880s, Jewish immigrants from Russia and Poland formed a second Jewish congregation in Wilmington. First organized as the B'nai Israel Society in 1898, the early congregation met in a member's home on Dock Street. The Orthodox congregation hired its first rabbi in 1907 and established a synagogue on Walnut Street in 1913. B'nai Israel eventually left downtown and constructed a new suburban synagogue in the mid-1950s. At the time of this move the synagogue affiliated itself with the Conservative movement in American Judaism.

In 1925 the First Presbyterian Church building, designed by Samuel Sloan in 1858, burned. Its replacement was designed by Hobart Upjohn in a Neo-Gothic style. This church, whose cornerstone was laid in 1927, was built in a basilica plan with a steeple and spire whose height gave added emphasis to its monumental style.

Records of Greek families in Wilmington date back to the late 1800s, many of them tracing their ancestry to the island of Ikaria. The Greek Vice-Consul for North and South Carolina made his home in Wilmington in 1911. The first Greek Orthodox Church (St. Nicholas) was dedicated in 1943 at the corner of Second and Orange Streets.

Amid the construction of new downtown churches, St. James was making additions to its church complex. The 1924 Parish Hall was designed by New York architect Hobart Upjohn. The St. James contract led to his work on First Presbyterian two years later.

ST. JAMES EPISCOPAL CHURCH

(Opposite page) The 1913 B'nai Israel Synagogue on Walnut Street (seen here shortly after its completion) was similar in scale to neighboring homes. The patterned brick face of the synagogue incorporated the Star of David into its masonry.

CFM IMAGE ARCHIVES

The cornerstone of St. Nicholas Greek Orthodox (left) at the corner of Second and Orange came at the completion of the structure in August 1945. The growing congregation sold the structure to St. John's Museum of Art in 1979. They now worship on College Road.

ST. NICHOLAS GREEK ORTHODOX CHURCH

A devastating 1925 New Year's Eve fire left the First Presbyterian congregation without a sanctuary. Hobart Upjohn, a specialist in ecclesiastical and collegiate architecture, was given the commission to design the congregation's new church at Third and Orange. His conception (shown here) for the French Neo-Gothic granite structure included a clock in the bell tower that was never installed.

FIRST PRESBYTERIAN CHURCH

ARCHITECTS

Numerous examples of Wilmington's historic religious structures were designed by architects recognized widely for their skill and innovation. Even as Wilmington produced its own capable architects and builders, local congregations were aware of trend-setting new projects on the national level. Throughout the 19th and the early 20th century, several influential architects were commissioned to work in Wilmington.

Thomas U. Walter

Born in 1804 and named a professor of architecture at the Franklin Institute in 1841, Walter was well-known for his Greek Revival Girard College for Orphans, his extension and dome on the United States Capitol, and his work on the United States Treasury building. Adept at interpreting Greek, Gothic, and Italianate styles, Walter's 1838 plan for St. James Episcopal was one of his many church designs. Walter died in 1887.

Architect of the Capitol

Thomas U. Walter

William Ralph Emerson

Related distantly to Ralph Waldo Emerson, William Ralph Emerson was born in Illinois in 1833. Best known as a residential designer, he is credited with innovating the Shingle style. Emerson helped establish the Boston Society of Architects and worked with Carl Fehmer, another well-known Boston architect, from 1864 to 1873. During the partnership with Fehmer, Emerson was involved in the design of St. Mark's Episcopal Church.

Maine Historic Preservation Commission

William Ralph Emerson

Almost all of his work is located in the northeastern United States. The design for St. Mark's is one of Emerson's few Southern projects.

Rafael Guastavino, Sr.*, and *Rafael Guastavino, Jr.

The elder Guastavino was born in Valencia, Spain, in 1842 and immigrated to the United States with his son in 1881. Together, the Guastavinos perfected their system of cohesive construction with thin masonry vaulting and remark-

Columbia University, Avery Architectural & Fine Arts Library

Rafael Guastavino, Sr.

Columbia University, Avery Architectural & Fine Arts Library

Hobart B. Upjohn

able weight-bearing capacity. The Guastavinos participated in the construction of more than 200 churches, cathedrals, and campus chapels, as well as working on the Boston Public Library, the Smithsonian Museum, and the Biltmore Estate in Asheville, North Carolina. The elder Guastavino died in Asheville in 1908 and his son in Bayshore, Long Island in 1950.

Hobart B. Upjohn

The son and grandson of architects, Hobart B. Upjohn was born in Brooklyn, New York in 1876. His grandfather, Richard Upjohn, a well-known architect of the Gothic Revival style in America, designed Trinity Church in New York City. Hobart Upjohn also established a reputation as a church architect. His work in Wilmington included the Church of the Good Shepherd, First Presbyterian, and The Great Hall of St. James. He also designed a new Chapel of the Cross in Chapel Hill, Temple Emanuel and First Presbyterian in Greensboro, and the Library at North Carolina State University. Upjohn died in 1949.

Samuel Sloan

Born in Pennsylvania in 1815 and associated with Philadelphia for much of his career, Samuel Sloan made his early reputation designing hospitals for the insane. By the 1850s, Sloan had expanded his architectural focus to include churches. A favorite architect among Baptists and Presbyterians, he received more than a dozen major commissions from these denominations. Besides First Baptist and First Presbyterian, Sloan designed the Bank of New Hanover in Wilmington, and recent evidence suggests that he may have designed the Temple of Israel. In 1883 he moved his office from Philadelphia to Raleigh. He died in 1884 while at work on a Morganton, North Carolina, project. No image of Sloan is known to exist.

Early Suburbs

Facilitated by the extension of streetcar lines and the growth of a prosperous middle class in Wilmington, suburbs such as Carolina Place, Carolina Heights, and Winoca Terrace were developed in the early twentieth century.

While Mary Baker Eddy, the founder of the Christian Science religion, lived in Wilmington briefly in 1844, it wasn't until 1895 that the state's first Christian Science Reading Room was established. In 1907 the First Church of Christ, Scientist's Neo-Classical structure was built on Market Street. In 1923, the structure was sold to a Baptist congregation and the Christian Science congregation moved to a new church, also built in a Neo-Classical style, on Chestnut Street.

With its pedimented portico and tall columns, Temple Baptist seemed a fitting name for the congregation that purchased the Christian Science church building. The Baptists worshipped in the structure until it was destroyed in a 1952 fire. The congregation rebuilt a block away on Market Street the following year.

Neo-Classicism is also evident in the architecture of Trinity Methodist Church, with its monumental portico entrance supported by Corinthian columns. The congregation first organized in 1889 as a Sunday School in the Giblem Masonic Lodge. It grew and formed the Market Street Methodist Church first located on Eighth and later on Ninth Street. The congregation changed its name to Trinity Methodist and in 1915 the suburban site at 14th and Market was acquired, the building completed in 1921.

Pearsall Memorial Presbyterian Church, named for the donor of the land and the building, was organized in 1914 as a church for suburban East Wilmington. The brick structure employed a modified Romanesque design.

The Church of the Covenant, built in an English Gothic Revival form, was organized in 1917 at the corner of 15th and Market. In 1944, the St. Andrews Presbyterian congregation left downtown and merged with the suburban Church of the Covenant to form St. Andrews-Covenant Presbyterian Church.

St. Andrew's-Covenant Presbyterian at Fifteenth and Market had its beginning in 1917 as the Church of the Covenant. The complex of Neo-Gothic structures includes the Kenan Memorial Building from 1921 by architects K.M. Murchison and James Gause. A 1920 article in the ***Presbyterian Standard*** *proclaimed the original sanctuary to be "one of the most unique works of architecture in the South." The Church of the Covenant merged with St. Andrew's Presbyterian in 1944.*

NHCPL Local History Room

Architect Leslie Boney, Sr. designed the 1921 Neoclassical style Trinity Methodist Church at Fourteenth and Market for W. J. Wilkins and Co. of Wilmington. The firm also designed the adjacent New Hanover High School during the same period.

TRINITY METHODIST CHURCH

Market Street Methodist, first at Eighth and Market, then Ninth and Market, grew from an 1889 Sunday school in the Giblem Masonic Lodge. The congregation eventually changed their name to Trinity and left the Ninth Street location (right) when their new church was complete.

TRINITY METHODIST CHURCH

Above: This Neoclassical style structure, built in 1907 by the Church of Christ, Scientist, stood at the corner of Seventeenth and Market. It served the Christian Scientists until it was sold in 1923 to Temple Baptist Church. In 1952, the building was destroyed by fire. Both congregations who used this columned church rebuilt within a few blocks of their original location, the Christian Scientists' new building (left) was completed in 1928, Temple Baptist's structure (below) was completed in 1953.

Above and Left: NHCPL Local History Room
Right: Temple Baptist Church

Left: The 1914 Pearsall Memorial Church incorporates design elements of English country churches and the Romanesque. It was constructed as a memorial to Rachel Pearsall by her husband Oscar.

RACHEL TURNER

St. Paul's Episcopal left their Fourth and Orange location in 1914 when their new suburban Neo-Gothic church was completed at Sixteenth and Market. The original structure (right) faced Sixteenth Street. It was later incorporated into a larger complex of church structures. Elements of the chancel were re-used from the Fourth Street church.

ST. PAUL'S EPISCOPAL CHURCH

FURTHER SUBURBANIZATION

The modest brick church built by the Wesley Memorial Methodist congregation in 1917 was replaced by this 1956 sanctuary (above).

WESLEY MEMORIAL METHODIST CHURCH

The road to Wrightsville Beach once was paved with discarded oyster shells, but by 1910 passengers shuttled by rail service between the beach and downtown Wilmington. The Winter Park suburb, which grew up adjacent to these transportation lines, soon supported three churches.

Begun as a Baptist mission Sunday School, Winter Park Baptist's original 1911 building was replaced in 1926. By 1956, as the congregation continued to grow, a remodeling of the sanctuary occurred, one which continued the Classical form of the earlier building, accentuating it with a pedimented portico and a tall steeple.

The Classical Revival also shaped Winter Park Presbyterian Church. Also begun as a Sunday School mission and then organized formally as a congregation in 1913, the first church was dedicated in March 1916. This building, with Ionic columns supporting a pedimented portico and topped by a cupola, was destroyed by fire in January 1939. Another church was built in the same style and on the same location within the following year.

Organized in 1914 as the Winter Park Methodist Episcopal Church, South, the congregation changed its name in 1916 to Wesley Memorial Methodist Church. A simple brick church was completed by 1917. The 1956 widening of an adjacent street into Highway 132 necessitated a new house of worship. The new building, an English Gothic design, hosted its first services by June of the same year.

Neither Neo-Gothic nor Classical Revival, the 1924 St. Andrews-On-the-Sound Episcopal Church was built in the Spanish Colonial Mission style, popular in California, Florida, and elsewhere in the nation during the 1920s. The church incorporates a characteristic tile roof, scalloped gable ends, and broad unbroken exterior surfaces of rough cement stucco.

The Sunset Park suburb on the southern edge of the city was established in 1912. Envisioned as a planned community, this subdivision experienced growth in 1918 from its proximity to the Liberty and Carolina shipyards and saw renewed activity in 1941 when the North Carolina Shipyards began building Liberty ships. Responding to the residential and military growth, Baptist and Methodist churches were organized. Begun in a tent in 1942, Sunset Park Baptist Church completed a new building in 1951. Sunset Park Methodist Church began holding services in February 1943. By October 1954 a new sanctuary had been completed.

Presbyterians established a presence in the Winter Park community with a Sunday School mission (below) in 1913. The first frame structure served the congregation until a brick Classical Revival church (left) was dedicated in 1916. After a 1939 fire destroyed this building, it was rebuilt in a similar design .

FIRST PRESBYTERIAN CHURCH AND WINTER PARK BAPTIST CHURCH

Winter Park Baptist formed in 1911 as a mission and Sunday school. By 1926 a new Classical Revival structure (at left in the image) was built. Through the years numerous additions joined the building to a larger church complex.

WINTER PARK BAPTIST CHURCH

This early 1950's aerial view of Winter Park shows all three suburban churches: (A) Winter Park Presbyterian, (B) Wesley Memorial Methodist, and (C) Winter Park Baptist. Note that current day College Road (SW to NE diagonally) ends at Wrightsville Avenue.

CHARLIE RIVENBARK

The 1924 St. Andrew's on-the-Sound Episcopal Church is the only Spanish Colonial Mission style house of worship in the area. Designed by Leslie Boney, Sr., it was built to serve the summer residents of the Greenville, Wrightsville, and Masonboro Sound areas.

NHCPL LOCAL HISTORY ROOM, LOUIS T. MOORE COLLECTION

Because of Sunset Park's proximity to Wilmington's shipyards, the suburb experienced dramatic growth during WWII. Methodist and Baptist congregations initially held services in temporary structures until more permanent buildings could be erected. Sunset Park Baptist (below) was completed in 1951 and Sunset Park Methodist (right) was completed in 1943.

GRACE METHODIST CHURCH & SUNSET PARK BAPTIST CHURCH

EPILOGUE

Since the end of World War II, significant trends have emerged. In 1950 the population of Wilmington was 45,000 and New Hanover County had about 100 religious groups. By 1998 the population had topped 64,000 and the number of religious groups in the county was over 230. Charismatic and non-denominational groups, Islamic and Buddhist congregations and ministries to non-English speaking communities all joined traditional churches and synagogues in making up the Cape Fear religious scene. New residents – retirees from other parts of the United States and immigrants from other parts of the world – started congregations and built new churches, contributing to the the impressive legacy of architecture and religion in Wilmington.

NHCPL, Local History Room, Fales Collection

Walking tour of historic churches in downtown Wilmington

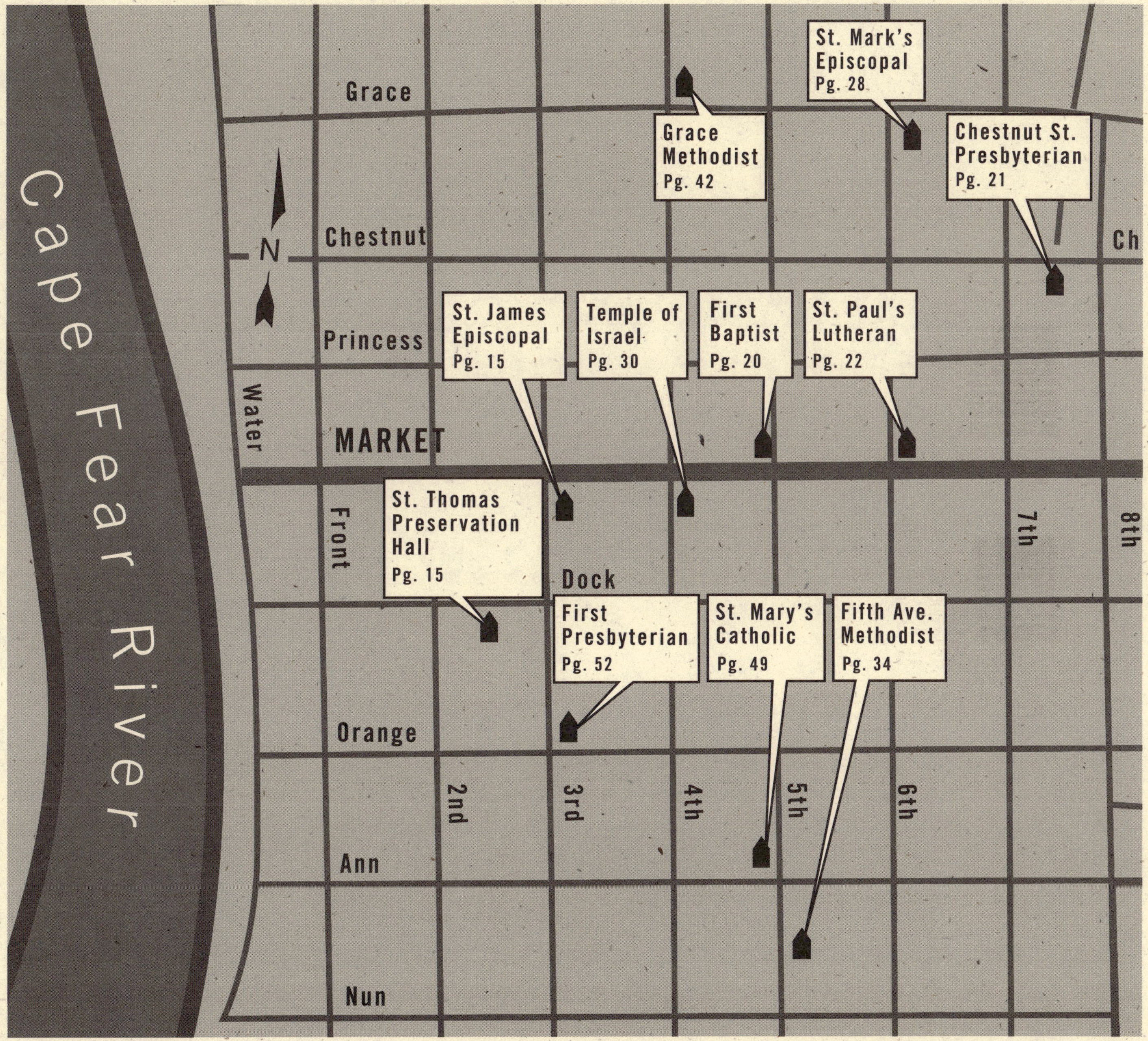

The eleven churches illustrated in the map represent a sampling of Wilmington's religious architecture...within walking distance in the downtown historic district. For more information on the individual religious institutions, please refer to the listed page number. Generally, only the building exteriors are available for viewing.